THE
PERILS OF FLIGHT

Originally published in France in 1911.
First published in the United States 1979 by
Mayflower Books, Inc., New York City 10022.
Text © Ernest Benn Limited 1978 – London & Tonbridge.
Illustrations © Garnier Frères 1978 – Paris.
after the original edition published by Garnier Frères in 1911.

Library of Congress Cataloging in Publication Data
Xaudaro, J
Perils of Flight
1. Aeronautics—Pictorial works. I. Title.
TL549.X38   629.13'02'07   78-24054
ISBN 0 8317 6810 X
Printed in Italy by Sagdos S.p.A.
Brugherio (MI).
First American Edition.

J. XAUDARO

THE

PERILS

OF

FLIGHT

MAYFLOWER BOOKS, INC.,
575 LEXINGTON AVENUE,
NEW YORK CITY 10022.

Witches are believed to have been the first to see the possibilities of airborne travel.

Don Quixote was another pioneer.

Pegasus, too, was an early aviator.

But we have good reason to believe that the airplane was in existence in prehistoric times.

Once the young pilot had grasped the laws of gravity . . .

. . . he could, thanks to this ingenious device, reach the most dizzy heights in safety . . .

. . . and, after very few training sessions, he could stay airborne even in the most turbulent conditions.

The only thing remaining was to master the difficult technique of landing.

Here he is, successfully airborne, watched enviously by a couple of would-be pilots.

There are three types of disaster;
Personal disaster.

Structural disaster only
(very rare).

Total disaster
(much more common).

Far superior to trains for speed and safety are the machines which have been designed specially for those who like to travel in comfort.

A public place seen from the air.

Marius' first flight. Let's hope they don't need the shovel!

Animals (all together): "It must be one of those French birds!"

Early Spanish aviators were not always skillful in their choice of landing sites.

Even if aviators could sometimes laugh at the efforts of birds of prey . . .

. . . on other occasions they felt less secure.

Volcanoes were obviously intended to be used as cigarette lighters.

Travelling by air meant a whole new set of hazards.

Trees caused special problems, both for the pilot . . . and for those underneath.

Inflatable clothing could be used in the event of an accident . . .

. . . while peaceful citizens could wear specially adapted shock-absorbers.

1. Before   2. After

Warning: never take on board any passenger likely to be seasick.

Just as there are sirens on the sea, so there are will o'the wisps in the air
ready to lure the unwary to their doom.

Telephone wires can sometimes act as a safety-net.

A steeple is not generally the most comfortable of places to land.

Thanks to the air-express, New York is only 1½ hours from London.
Price of a one-way trip: $1000 (disaster inclusive).

For those who might find this figure on the high side, the air-express is equipped with
every modern convenience and travellers are treated with the utmost respect.

Stations have, of course, changed a little . . .

. . . and travellers are charged according to weight.

As a safety precaution, the S.P.A. (Society for the Protection of Aviators) has designed
a new kind of shock-absorber based on the principle of the mattress.

While it is unlikely that the airplane will ever replace the taxi . . .

. . . air routes may become congested with the fashion-conscious, all in their latest 200 H.P. models . . .

. . . making it possible to sip a cocktail in the air just as pleasantly
as in a café.

The airborne duel is, naturally enough, incredibly dangerous, especially for the seconds.

Airborne Pigeon Post calls for a certain finesse.

Removals to and from any country by charter plane. Reliability assured.

An airplane adapted for the hunt.

Caught in the act!

Drought has become a thing of the past, thanks to air-spray.

The winner of the Grand Prix.

The departure of the Biskra-Timbuctoo Airbus.

For the future, even flying fish may have possibilities . . .